THE ISLE OF
ORLEANS

TROMBONE
SOLO

MUSIC MINUS ONE

3933

SUGGESTIONS FOR USING THIS MMO EDITION

WE HAVE TRIED to create a product that will provide you an easy way to learn and perform these compositions with a full ensemble in the comfort of your own home. Because it involves a fixed accompaniment performance, there is an inherent lack of flexibility in tempo. The following MMO features and techniques will reduce these inflexibilities and help you maximize the effectiveness of the MMO practice and performance system:

We have observed generally accepted tempi, and always in the originally intended key, but some may wish to perform at a different tempo, or to slow down or speed up the accompaniment for practice purposes; or to alter the piece to a more comfortable key. We have included slow-tempo versions of the most up-tempo pieces on this album for practice and/or a slower interpretation. But for even more flexibility, you can purchase from MMO specialized CD players & recorders which allow variable speed while maintaining proper pitch, and vice versa. This is an indispensable tool for the serious musician and you may wish to look into purchasing this useful piece of equipment for full enjoyment of all your MMO editions.

We want to provide you with the most useful practice and performance accompaniments possible. If you have any suggestions for improving the MMO system, please feel free to contact us. You can reach us by e-mail at info@musicminusone.com.

3933

CONTENTS

ISBN 1-59615-105-6

Magnolia Dance

Tim Laughlin

Trombone

Blues for Faz

Tim Laughlin

MMO 3933

Trombone

Suburban St. Parade

Tim Laughlin

MMO 3933

MMO 3933

Gentilly Strut

Tim Laughlin

I Know I'll See You Again

Tim Laughlin

Crescent City Moon

Tim Laughlin

Isle of Orleans

Tim Laughlin

Monkey Hill

Tim Laughlin

DIXIELAND ENSEMBLE---PLAY TWO TIMES ---TAILGATE

129

133

137

141

145

149

153

158

MMO 3933

MUSIC MINUS ONE
50 Executive Boulevard
Elmsford, New York 10523-1325
1.800.669.7464 (U.S.)/914.592.1188 (International)

www.musicminusone.com
e-mail: mmogroup@musicminusone.com